LIFE
on the
EDGE
of TIME

David Wilkerson

LIFE ON THE EDGE OF TIME

Fleming H. Revell Company
Old Tappan, New Jersey

Library of Congress Cataloging in Publication Data

Wilkerson, David R.
    Life on the edge of time.

    Poems.
    I. Title.
PS3573.14355L5   811'.5'4   72–4088
ISBN 0–8007–0553–X

CONTENTS

Special thanks to
Bob Summers
for helping me put this book
into final manuscript form.
His research and hard work
were invaluable.

TO

My Wife Gwen

THE WOMAN I LOVE

≈≈≈≈≈≈≈≈≈≈≈≈≈≈≈≈≈≈≈≈≈≈≈≈≈≈≈≈≈≈≈≈≈≈

She embodies concepts and attitudes
Appealing especially to me—
> Her walk,
> Her smile,
> Her hair,
> Her style,
> Her cool way.

The way she can, without words,
> Appreciate my return smile.

She has a humble pride in being herself:
> Being involved.

She wears an inescapable identity.
> Her expression,
> Her compassion,
> Are balanced by inner joy.

She knows who she is,

Where she is going,
And how to get there.
Really contemporary:
So much with it!
She can be truly romantic
Showing a sense of need for her man.
She has a passionate concern
To make things just right for him:
Spends no time drifting around in her head
Trying to find herself.
She is aware, but not worried,
Because she is totally given to a cause
(And reminded of that cause
Every time she looks into my eyes).
She is motivated by my pride in her—
Which is mirrored in these eyes.
She is
Direct,
Assured,
A little aloof
To those who do not know her well,
(Never unreachable to those who touch her soul).

She is sexy in a stirring and feminine way!
>> Because of her heritage of living
>> With reality,
She knows that a loving woman
>> Can be a partner to a man with ideals
>> And still be treated like a woman.
She is human: earthy but divinely sensitive!
>> She identifies with now, not some neurosis.
She turns me on because her spirit is on fire.
>> Her ceaseless drive is purposeful.
>> And her laughter is contagious.
When she walks down the street everybody notices.
>> She is ready for the challenge of every glance.
She makes me glad
>> That I am a man and she is a woman.
She has confidence,
>> And it's contagious.
She has energy,
>> And I tune in on every channel.
She is aware of the wide world,
>> But makes me know it's just the two of us.
She is a teacher of other women.

LIFE ON THE EDGE OF TIME

There is no crisis of identity,
>   For she has found the spring
>   Of life in Christ.
She is for real:
>   Not plastic or unreachable.
She is beauty.
>   She loves well and true—
>   Deeply and fully.
She makes God seem near
>   (Because just the thought of her
>   Is better than the touch of another).
The bond is eternal.
>   She turns me on—
>   Only she can turn me off.
She's my girl—my woman!

LIFE ON THE EDGE OF TIME

Life is now a base camp on the edge of time,
      A platform for mounting expeditions
            into the origins of existence.
To learn how to be born again
      One assumes the possibility of getting lost
            without becoming a casualty.
But the stresses of the sixties changed all that
      When young people began to eat
            the fruit of drugs and revolution.
Perhaps it started when the Kennedy laughter was cut off
      By bullets: when our nation became expert
            at staging state funerals.
The summer of love was replaced by the winter of speed.
      Original hippies of Haight disappeared
            into the desert!
Teeny-boppers began looking
      For holes to hide in.
            Splitting and shivering became epidemic.

For those who walk in darkness
Both in the day time and in the night time
The right time and right place are not here.

                              —T. S. Eliot

They went to the Indian to learn how to live off the land,
        Communes sprang up like emergency wards
                for emaciated victims!
They were saying it with flowers,
        But no one knew
                they were funeral flowers!
Life became boring, ugly, senseless,
        Death seemed so satisfying,
                pontifical and symbolic rhetoric
                replaced wisdom.
A New Left developed,
        Baited by Herbert Marcuse and his Marxist theory,
        They flocked to hear
        "CAPITALISM IS COLLAPSING!"
The most wanted high-school radicals
        Sporting around in wire-wheeled Triumphs
                and silky puff-sleeved shirts experienced

> political orgasms with revolutionary
> vibrations.

> Caught in the sensual music, all ne-
> glect monuments of unaging intellect.

>> —W. B. Yeats, prophet and
>> 1923 Nobel Prize recipient

But the new revolutionary is antiintellectual
    Burning libraries
        and boycotting classes.
The New Left prefers the thrill of activist phrases
    Like—UNDERMINE THE FOUNDATIONS OF
THE SYSTEM
        and LIBERATE ALL INSTINCTUAL
        NEEDS
Proof enough of the failure of the philosophers
    To the Right and Left
        who have done little more than repeat
        what has already been said!

    Songs, chants, and slogans of the Slavic people while
    princes and Lord are captive in the prisons in the

future, by idiots without heads will be received as
divine oracles.

Nostradamus, the prophet, 1555

But this is not the time to die.
>It is time to live
>>and only in Him is the source of life!

JESUS CHRIST—SOLID ROCK!
>He bridges the gap between time and eternity
>>revealing the secret all men now seek:
>>How to be born again.

Getting into Him makes it happen.
>Man becomes a new creation.
>>The old man with his hang-ups vanishes.

A NEW MAN IS BORN
>Timeless and eternal—
>>who will never die!

Revolution is transitory and weak.
>Jesus Christ brings restoration:
>>Something no revolution has ever done.

Initiation into the restoration movement is only by
DEATH—

To self, to pride, to sin,
      to the world.
Total realization and eternal freedom is the reward.
    Answer that—if you can,
      Herbert Marcuse!

About the Time of the End, a body of men will be raised up who will turn to the Prophecies, and insist upon their literal interpretations, in the midst of much clamor and opposition.

—Sir Isaac Newton, 300 years ago

THE BEAST, THE OWL, AND
THE DRAGON

~~~~~~

. . . the clocks were striking thirteen.

—George Orwell, *1984*

It was a decade of disaster:
>   Revolutions broke out everywhere.
The middle-class home began to fall apart:
>   Establishment churches couldn't hold their young.
Schools became centers of rebellion:
>   Streets were battlegrounds between black and
>   white—
>   Sit-ins, shut-outs, and sabotage!
Clothes became freaky and funky:
>   Young men burned draft cards.
Vietcong flags were waved:
>   The stars and stripes were spat upon.
Seduced by acid music, pot, and smut
>   The dissenters got mad at the Establishment.

The moping owl does to the moon complain.

—Thomas Gray

(And Establishment powers retaliated.)
Heroes were the Beatles, the Fugs, and Ginsberg:
    Truly antihero imposters.
Leftist fought Rightist:
    Students fought the police.
Police struck for higher wages:
    Teachers locked out students.
Hard-hats dumped sewage into the rivers:
    Locked up bridges and barricaded waterfronts.
    (While hippies refused to work)
    Those who worked got greedy.
Veterans returned as junkies:
    Vietnam turned father against son.
The silent majority wanted a piece of the action:
    While the beast, the owl, and the dragon had their
        day.
Remember how the prophet Isaiah predicted
    The owl and the dragon would be converted
    And honor God.

LIFE ON THE EDGE OF TIME
〰〰〰〰〰〰〰〰〰〰〰〰〰〰〰〰〰〰〰〰

The brute beast is described by Peter (2 Peter 2)
> As one who despises the government:
>> Proud and self-willed,
>> Not afraid to speak evil of dignitaries
>> Rioting in the daytime,
>> Eyes full of adultery,
>> Beguiling unstable souls,
>> Servants of corruption,
>> Walking in the lusts of uncleanness.

Yet the prophet predicted these rebels would return
> To honor and glorify God.

The prophet Joel added,
> "The beasts of the field will cry also unto thee. . . ."

Along with the owl
> (Representing the lonely who walk at night).

Job, in his loneliness and despair cried—
> "I am . . . a companion to owls."

These are souls dangling on the brink of suicide:

Men may live fools, but fools they cannot die.

—Edward Young

LIFE ON THE EDGE OF TIME

Runaways and nightwalkers,
Prostitutes and lonely souls without friendship!
The owls will be restored to honor the Lord.
The dragons also turn homeward
—Not the old dragon, Satan—
But those Satan has deceived and hooked
With alcohol, perversion, and drugs.
(I have visited in the den of those dragons;
While they spat their ghastly fire of fear,
Observed the smoke of their torment ascending
upwards,
And smelled the breath of restless nights and
empty days.)
Abused and buffeted by hell,
They too will come back to our Lord,
And honor Him as the psalmist prophesied:
"Praise the Lord from the earth,
ye dragons and all deeps. . . ."
God promised to visit this Now generation,
Living on the edge of time!
He promised to make a way in their wilderness:
Rivers in their deserts!

LIFE ON THE EDGE OF TIME

Things are changing: Jesus is *in*.

    The Holy Ghost has come *down*.

    Not just a well springing *up*.

    But rivers that flow—waters to wash *in*.

God said, "I will do a new thing. . . ."

    And so He has!

A vibrant twentieth-century church is being born,

    Led by youth who have jettisoned heavy prejudices

To gather in open fields and on seashores

    Singing:

    "Blest be the tie that binds Our hearts in Christian
      love."

    (While church dignitaries wave

    Their own denominational banners).

Protestants are beginning to love the Catholics:

    It no longer matters what church you belong to:

    The new Jesus People are even praying

    For the communists, too—

    (They still despise the doctrine of Marx and Lenin,

    But believe God's promise to pour out His Spirit

    Upon all flesh—including those in Iron Curtain
      countries:

    The Russians, Chinese, Albanians, and Hungarians.)

LIFE ON THE EDGE OF TIME

These new Christians hate lukewarm*ism* worse than any *ism*.
    The prophet Isaiah saw our day and prophesied:
        Prayerlessness in the house of Jacob,
        Weariness and fatigue in Israel,
        A begrudging of tithes and sacrifices,
        Love of ease and materialism,
        Covetousness and sensuality,
        A winking at sin and compromise,
        Profaning of God's Word and His
          commandments!
The irony of it all is clear:
    While the saints grow weary and weak,
    The beast, the owl, and the dragon
        Press into the kingdom!

    The worm of conscience is the companion of the owl.
    The light is shunned by sinners. . . .

                    —Schiller

And the established church is now in danger
    Of missing the move of God.
A generation that has cursed the church is returning—
    Not to organized worship and dead liturgy,

But to the worship of the Man, Jesus Christ.
Welcome back!
>   To all the beasts,
>   All the owls,
>   All the dragons.

THE ROTTEN APPLE CORE

I remember the day the Beatles "happened."
      Suddenly the Beatles *were*!
And they became a part of our environment,
      Like TV and credit cards.
We adjusted to them,
      Laughed at their innocent jesting with the press,
But worried about the biological attraction of their sound
      And their unknown, ominous charisma.
Now the Beatles are aging children
      Fighting over a rotting Apple Core Corporation.
They are, you see, over thirty.
      Once they said they were better known
Than Jesus Christ.
      But today they waddle in submission;
      They didn't even leave a monument.

      I sing of autumn and the falling fruit
      And the long journey towards oblivion.

The apples falling like great drops of dew
To bruise themselves an exit from themselves.

The whole trip has been flushed:
        Many of those Beatle fans moved on
        Becoming civil rights activists and peaceniks.
Others turned to dope and acid music,
        One hundred sixty-eight million dollars later!
They themselves disappeared down Abbey Road.
        Age has a way of collecting its dues:
        It marks us well

        Quietus is the goal of the long journey,
        The longest journey towards oblivion.

And the poor lads have to pay up.
        They tumbled off their plateau,
        Their drums have been silenced.
All you can hear is an echo—
        Just one line from their most famous song:
        "I don't know—I don't know."

It's hard to believe
>These aging men were once merely boys
>Caught up in a public relations dream.
Actually they were crushed by Rolling Stones,
>Who in turn were shut out by The Doors,
>Who were zapped by The Mothers of Invention.
While the Jesus Restoration Movement sweeps over the
Earth
>And thousands of former Beatlemaniacs turn to
>Christ
Little children look up and ask:
>"What's a Beatle?"

>Oh pity the dead that are dead
>But cannot take the journey.

The quotations in the above poem are from "Ship of Death" by
D. H. Lawrence.

OPEN LETTER TO CAMPUS REBELS

When hopes and dreams are loose in the streets, it
is well for the timid to lock doors, shutter windows,
and lie low until the wrath has passed. For there is
often a monstrous incongruity between the hopes,
however noble and tender, and the action which
follows them.

—Eric Hoffer

Attention, all runaways and rebels!
>   You do your thing
>   And I'll do mine.
And what is my thing?
>   I like to preach the Word.
There is a wild, fantastic something in me
>   That wants to come out.
I've got a message all pent up inside.
>   I'm going to let it out,

Line by line—
So that it can go down easy.
HERE GOES:
You say, "Destroy the American system:
It has not abolished unemployment and war."
Then you must blow up the hospitals:
They have not abolished cancer.
You want to make revolution,
Then find out what for!
The Establishment is supposed to be against the poor.
Yet poverty in America is on the decline.
In 1900, about 90 percent of our population was poor,
In 1920, 50 percent,
In 1930, 34 percent,
In 1968, only 15 percent.
The job is far from finished,
But don't say someone is not trying.
Now who has failed?
You have.
You fail because you no longer
Want to think.
You fail by using violence
To shut down schools.

You fail by denying freedom to some
      While you cry freedom for all.
You slander and abuse anyone
      Who disagrees with you.
You steal, loot administration buildings,
      And defy all authority—
Then try to whitewash your ignorance with idealism
      And call your hysteria insight!
You say, "The American people demand. . . ."
      Then you add only what you want.
Really now:
      This is intellectual sloppiness!
So you want to wreck the system.
      It took centuries of pain and suffering
      To devise democracy:
A system
      That protects squares like me from rebels like you;
      That protects innocents like you from fascists;
A system
      That still protects every minority from tyranny;
A system
      That at least tries to solve human problems;

A system

> That still seeks to make changes without violence;

A system

> That abhors bloodshed;

A system

> That refuses to suppress free speech;

The only system

> That allows reckless attacks against itself
> And allows mass demonstrations
> To be nationally televised—

And you want to smash it!

> What would you give us in its place?
> "Heroes" such as Marx, Mao, and Che?

Leaders who demand power

> While jailing students, writers, scientists, teachers,
> Banishing them to labor or death—
> Only because of their opinions?

Tanks and armies rolling over borders

> To "liberate"?

You plan to give us

> Nonviolent coordinating committees
> Who engage in gunfire and violence!

LIFE ON THE EDGE OF TIME

You would dig out of the grave
        A nineteenth-century ideology: Marxism!
You would give us assertions
        And deny us facts!
Passion as a substitute for knowledge,
        Slogans for solutions:
Idealism with absolutely no realism behind it!
NO, thank you, my rioting student friends.
Whatever its imperfections, give me democracy.

      I ask for, not at once no government, but at *once* a
      better government.

                                    —Thoreau

I despise poverty more than you,
        But I am free to give.
I despise pompous politicians,
        But not one of them
        Has my back against the wall.
The smugly affluent bug me too:
        But God help us if we didn't have their taxes to
          feed the poor.

Sure, I know there is a credibility gap,
       But it beats having to swallow
       A dogma enforced by terror.
Under democracy I am a free man:
       Free to worship God,
       (Even to the point of fanaticism).
Free to stand on any street corner in America
       And preach any gospel
Under the protection of a flag
       And a constitution.
Free to travel
       To any point on the globe.
Free to vote against inferior products
       Through dollar power,
And against dishonest politicians
       With my ballot.
Rebels so far have done little more
Than to soften the system.
They have blown kids' minds!
Frightened the conforming classes!
Questioned the legitimacy of everything.
Carved up capitalism
       Without the foggiest idea where to go.

LIFE ON THE EDGE OF TIME

It is more a shoddy revolution
>> Of jargon, slogans, and polysyllables
>> Than of substantial ideas.

Radicals and militants are now addicted
>> To the capitalist telephone.

They accept invitations to speak
>> And the money pours in.

They become capitalists,
>> Defanged by the dollar.

For one thousand dollars they will curse capitalism,
>> For two thousand revile the President.

Why is everything happening now—and together?
>> A surplus of causes seems to exist.

People are desiring to maintain
>> A sense of their own importance,

Trying to find values
>> In a superorganized world of bigness.

Caught in vacuums of impersonality,
>> Tossing in seas of powerlessness,

Man is horribly aware he no longer influences
>> The very decisions affecting his life.

Man is a prisoner, a slave of the world, and his rule
is illusion.

—Bonhoeffer

Loving, honesty, caring have become corny.
    "Make love, not war" is no longer lofty idealism:
    It is merely a sex slogan.
Good taste is now bad style.
Self-indulgence has become freedom.
Welfare has become slavery.
Leisure has turned to loneliness.
Religion has become neuroticism.
Goodness is equated with weakness.
Honesty with stupidity.
Could it be, campus rebel,
    That you're really not doing your thing at all?
But that your thing
    Is doing you?
The only dignity you can give to doubt
    Is to wrap it in silence.

There is no bravery in preaching revolution
          Without purpose,
And overthrow
          Without follow-up.
So true revolution may never work in America.
          To be a revolutionary is
          To love your life enough to change it.
There are not enough of you left
          In love with God
          And life
          And fellow man.

MARIJUANA HEAVEN

In 'Nam's field
The grass grows
Between the graves
Rows on rows.

—War graffiti

The underground press is spreading the word:

If you missed out getting turned on to grass in high
school or college the service will now allow you
to continue your education—Vietnam is marijuana
heaven.

There you can buy pot already processed into cigarette form,
Ten to the pack, two hundred to the carton,
And one pack costs only a dollar.
In highland battlefields it grows wild.
Drug abuse in the service now involves thousands.

Lots of guys come over here very lame, but go home "heads." Guys have moustaches and long sideburns that the average citizen would never believe they were soldiers. We are anxious to get back and grow wild hair and beards without any restrictions. Beads and peace symbols are worn with the uniform.

—A Corporal in Phu Bai, Vietnam

Some officers blame the influence of rock music:

Rock and roll music contributes to both the usage of drugs and the high VD rate among the enlisted men in the army today.

—Army Captain

But the enlistee does not agree.
He believes the Vietnamese do not want him around
And besides, the war became an unbearable standoff.
So he gets away by getting stoned.
Almost every path is now littered
With marijuana cigarette butts.

Unlimited supplies, pot and opium, is all they have here. Out of six hundred men a good solid half, maybe more, get stoned on J's regularly. Many of them on opium. A regular practice is to blow outside the barracks, listen to some music, rap awhile, then go walking and blowing. You see GI's walking around blowing all the time. . . .

—A Corporal writing from Vietnam

Recruits complain army jobs are so intellectually easy
It is possible to stay stoned all the time,
(Which many now do, weeks on end).

Grass is so plentiful and cheap. LSD comes from the U.S. Occasionally we have Afghani and Pakistani hashish, and even sometimes we get "meth." Opium is plentiful. We take or smoke anything we can. I'm stoned 50 percent of my waking hours. War? What war?

—SP/4 writing from a mountain stonghold in Vietnam

LIFE ON THE EDGE OF TIME

Convicted drug users face discharge,
But most often it is not dishonorable—
Rather, administrative.
Cases are reported of soldiers provoking a bust
In order to get out of serving.

I say it's time this nation takes inventory,
Because enlisted men make up a lot of people
Trapped in a nasty and confusing dilemma,
A middle-of-the-road policy
Making olive drab prisoners out of soldiers.
Remember our boys:
Don't get down on them.
We have given them no true cause,
No reason to crusade.
Instead we ask them to serve with numb obedience
In a current war
That has little meaning!
Because no conclusions are expected:

> I guess about the only thing that really messes my
> mind is the thought of how foolish this whole ordeal is.
> Everyday I see evidence that indicates the Vietnamese

people resent our presence. If they don't want us, and we don't want to be here, just what the hell gives?

—An MP from Vietnam

Take up our quarrel with the foe:
To you from failing hands we throw
   The torch; be yours to hold it high!
   If ye break faith with us who die
We shall not sleep, though poppies grow
   In Flanders fields.

—John McCrae

LIFE ON THE EDGE OF TIME

THE NOW GENERATION

The catchword of our time is NOW,
No one dares cling to yesterday.
I suppose it all started with violence:
The murdering of John F. Kennedy,
Moral grandeur vanishing, totally,
Vulgarizing the old system.
Convictions of conspiracy
Motivated half-educated minds to destroy, convulsively!
Leaders lost control,
Anarchy let loose, innocence died, quickly.
Convictions gave way to expediency
Living under the eye of television

    BIG BROTHER IS WATCHING YOU

                    —George Orwell

Life was lived secondhand.
Viewers became winner-lovers,

Loser-haters.
There is now a trend to tribal values,
A preference for the isolated
Delimited self-life.

> If you crash here you must be over 17 and help chop
> weeds. Do not eat the chickens if they are laying eggs!
>
> —Brother Bill, Drop City Commune

We live in a global village.
The old walls have tumbled:
Environment is total confusion.
Everything is looking primitive again: weeds where roses
    once grew,
The tribal adornment of the body is an obsession,
To put on ornaments—a reentry to the tribal way of life.
Men wear jewelry, beads, bells, and earrings.
Men and women dress alike,
Sporting hair dyes, cosmetics, and lace.
Bodies are painted
In effort to create a beast
So they can step into its skin.
This putting on of the beast is only

A desperate effort to lose identity and become detached!
Every costume of every era is now worn.
The NOW generation searches all history
For a sense of direction.

So sad, so fresh, the days that are no more.

—Tennyson

Clothes are no longer wrappers,
But an extension of one's skin—
The language of the soul.
Echoes from the pit of despair:
Images reflected from the mirror of the mind,
Revealing vibrations below the surface:
Undercurrents of desire, fear, passion, and pride.
Clothes now reflect smoldering emotions,
Exposing the roots of man's ultimate thoughts.
They weave their own styles
With the fabric of tormented imaginations.
Sloppy dress expresses a role to be played
By independent underdogs in personal freedom.
Contemporary fashions invite youth
To step inside themselves rather than keep in step.

LIFE ON THE EDGE OF TIME

It is an invitation to touch the soul
By letting it hang out.
Masks are featured protection
From the morbid stare of evil,
And there is no more looking one right in the eye.

> As I am forgotten,
> And would be forgotten,
> So I would forget.

> —T.S. Eliot

The NOW generation gazes in different directions
Like the Roman god Janus,
Only with eyes like flashlights turned off.
Fashions now have sounds and smells:
Colognes come in lime, peat, and leather.
The lived-in smell of unwashed clothes is hip.
Women glow like electric eels,
Imitating light bulbs, TV sets, and chandeliers.
Fashion today has become a kind of weaponry
To shock, seduce, and frighten!
The Lenin cap and Nehru jackets, once prison garb,
Are worn by this generation as badges of rebellion.

LIFE ON THE EDGE OF TIME

Fashion swingers are a new breed
Creating a centrifugal force
Sucking thousands of innocents into a whirlpool
Of madness, drugs, sex, and nothingness.
Let none forget—
In the last stage of the Roman Empire
Youths dressed and groomed themselves
In the style of barbarians,
Just before the fall.
Wear your clothes in good style,
But remember—
You are defining yourself!
You are saying something:
SPEAK THE TRUTH.

O for a man who is a *man*, and, as my neighbor says, has a bone in his back which you cannot pass your hand through! Our statistics are at fault: the population has been returned too large. How many *men* are there to a square thousand miles in this country? Hardly one.

—Thoreau

THE LITTLE OLD WINEMAKER

~~~~~~

The greedy money changers are back in the temple,
       Drowning out the prayer and almsgiving
       With sales campaigns.
These are the religious people who cry,
       "Put Christ back into Christmas."
Listen to their pious indignation about commercialism,
       Blaming merchandising Jews for making a big buck
       On the Christian manger.
I have but two words for that: *Bah, Humbug!*
       Certain church groups themselves are among
       The biggest hucksters in the land.
They own assets running into the tens of billions:
       Buildings,
       Stock holdings,
       Factories,
       Bakeries,
       Land investments,
       And the little old winemaker is a monk!

How dare they accuse others of cashing in on Christ,
>   When prelates and preachers can flimflam and
>   swindle
>   In the name of God;
When tax dollars can be demanded for private institutions
>   And every effort made to avoid paying taxes
>   On high profit-making businesses.
I ask—who then is the real religion huckster?
>   Not the tent revivalist collecting his share
>   From the few poor and black;
>   Not the merchant
>   Who dresses Christ in a Santa Claus suit;
>   Not the radio preacher
>   Peddling magic reducing belts.

>   Just send in your love offering of five dollars or
>   more. . . .

The real culprit is big, organized, respected religion.
God's Word rebukes them
>   For being rich,
>   Increased with goods,
>   In need of nothing.

The maharishis of India come to us wrapped in cheap linen
  Preaching asceticism and self-denial.
And in about as long as it takes to repeat ten mantras,
They head for home with the loot:
  Jewelry,
  Cadillacs,
  Stereos,
  Swiss bank accounts.
Sure, it's a fraud! Yes, it's robbery!
  But these bearded prophets are pantywaists—
  They are amateurs when it comes to God-fraud.
The professional money changers work within the law
  Building ecclesiastical empires,
  While posing as defenders of the faith once delivered.
They are as adept at putting together
  A portfolio of gilt-edged stocks:

CHURCH SELLS HOTEL FOR 9 MILLION

—Times Herald

As they are at quoting Scriptures to the masses
  About giving to help the poor.

LIFE ON THE EDGE OF TIME

These despoilers don't operate only on the last week of
    December.
        They are full-time Wall Streeters,
        Turning the lowly Nazarene
        Into a little old winemaker.

PASS GO. COLLECT $200.

THE "HI-THERE" KIDS

~~~~~~

KIDS BACK CLEAN 'GENE IN DEMO BID

—New York Times

The "Hi-there" kids once rang doorbells
  For Eugene McCarthy.
Now they are on the eco-trip.
  (The ecology publicists have attracted them
  Hoping to drain them of hostilities.)
Let us not forget these kids are concerned:
  They see the planet Earth
  As a reeking, obnoxious, open sewer,
  And are convinced it is almost too late to remedy it!
They believe government is too unresponsive,
  And owes too much to corporations
  To restore ecological balance.
Dodging, stalling, and empty promises
  Will soon turn off all the "Hi-there" kids.

No longer will they lend tireless support
> To the keep-everything-clean people.

> The exploited masses are the trees and the fish of the
> sea—not just the blacks and hippies and Chinese.

> > —Gary Snyder

Listen, these youths are seeking social impact.
> Ralph Nader knows it—
> But the church doesn't!

Think of a few million "Hi-there" kids
> Wanting to ring doorbells
> Anywhere.

Ready to take on even the big corporations.
> Concerned,
> Militant,
> Aggressive,
> > They'll fight for Indians,
> > For peace,
> > For equality,
> > For all kinds of rights!

And I say *that* energy must be harnessed
> By God's men, for God's work.

Organize them into CURE corps.
       Challenge them to quit using love
       Like a mustard plaster,
And instead—go wipe the sweat
       Off someone's brow.
Picture a world teeming with "Hi-there" kids,
       All wound up like toy militants,
       Running around in all directions,
       Winding down—
       Looking for a real cause!
And we ministers stand in our observation booths
       Making endless observations
       About their aimlessness and lack of direction,
When instead we should be rounding them up—
       And winding them ever tighter.
Show them a Christ of power and miracles.
       Lay on them a functioning faith!
Get back to the simplicity of gospel compassion.
       Give them a place in our ghettoes!
With two hots and a cot,
       —That's all they ask for,
Let them risk their lives:
       Back them with money and muscle.

LIFE ON THE EDGE OF TIME

Ask them to become miracle workers,
      Tell them the truth.
God has no time for the ordinary,
      cut-and-dried "Hi-there" kids—
      He wants youth who expect the impossible:
Who will use their divine dissatisfaction
      To make of themselves mountain movers!
God wants a new breed of Holy Ghost radicals
      Ready to challenge hell itself,
      To lay claim on the souls of lost men—
      To clean up cesspools of iniquity.
So hear me—all you "Hi-there" kids,
      You with the Colgate smiles
      And the front door manners,
      Come on down with me into Harlem.
Put away your badges and buttons.
      Lay down your flags and banners.
      There's a whole nation of ghetto kids
         Needing your help. . . .
         They need a big brother, a sister!
Those pathetic little black and white faces
      Accented with cold, runny noses
      (Beneath their searching eyes)

Will tear your heart,
    As they have torn mine.
Ecology? Clean the environment?!
It all begins here—
    In the kingdoms of the mind.
Christ is all in all—He is a new environment!

> "And he [Jesus] put his arms around them [the little children], laid his hands upon them, and blessed them." (NEB)

SEXUAL FREEDOM

OUR COMMUNAL GOAL—CONSTANT ORGASM

—Drop City

Sex is high on the world's cash commodities list!
Perversions are wrapped in sweet titles like CANDY,
Obscene books are sold in the name of truth and liberation,
Dirty book shops flourish openly.
    Signs read,

        FEE OF TWO DOLLARS FOR LOOKING
        AT MAGAZINES IF NO PURCHASE.

Clerks sit high up in observation perches
    Ready to cash in on eroticism.
Purchases are sealed in plain brown paper sacks.
Lewd weekly papers are peddled boldly.
Claiming to be crusaders, they assault ordinary decency.
    They feature four-letter words,

Unretouched photos of male and female nudes
In all sorts of positions.
Plastered on their covers are labels which read:

WARNING! ADULT SEX MATERIAL.
THIS LITERATURE NOT INTENDED FOR MINORS.
UNDER NO CIRCUMSTANCES ARE THEY TO VIEW IT,
POSSESS IT, OR PLACE ORDERS
FOR THE MERCHANDISE HEREIN OFFERED.

This notice exempts the publisher from court rulings,
    While guaranteeing sales to curious minors.
Some humans are not content with the arrangements of
    nature.
    The natural system of reproduction is working well.
Male and female are still naturally attracted to one another.
    Sex within marriage bonds has never lost
    Its intended effect.
What more do some people want?
    Complete sexual freedom?
They want to know about how other people indulge:
    To hear men talk about it,
    To see it or to see pictures of it.

This is more than an innocent biological interest.
> It is dirty and demonic!
The perversity of some sophisticated people
> Cannot be overestimated.
In certain fashionable circles today,
> It is popular to recite sequences from dirty novels.
Pseudointellectuals have developed an unbounding curiosity
> About the permutations
> And perverted combination of human sex.
They are encouraged by the public admissions
> Of those in best circles who boast
> They are not innocent of these immoral practices.
Most of the dirty books are produced by idiots
> For idiots!
But the message that runs through all pornography is the same:
> Old puritan bonds must be broken!
> Sexual freedom will at last set things right
> In our society!
Mixing pornographic pleasure with propagandistic messages,
> They will have us know civilization will rot and fall
> Unless homosexuals and sadists are granted status.

It is tragic that some Christians are now
       Browsing through pornography "To censor it."
They collect it
       "To be in a better position to burn it."
There is danger in spotless hearts taking a mental trip
       Through the spectacles of pornography.
It is the basest kind of dishonesty
       To defend pornography and dirty sex
       Under the guise of social criticism.
Filth is filth—no matter how it is packaged!
No matter how much it costs!
In spite of who pushes it!
       Smut pushers are cashing in
       On this generation's biggest hoax:
       The superhuman sexual deeds
       Portrayed in pornographic books and magazines
       Are stupid, mostly impossible, and seldom tried in
         real life.
       Seduction is related to drugs, force,
       Alcohol, brutality, and gimmickry.
       Essential elements include beatings, knifings,
         shootings.

The main characters are freakish,
Bisexual, demonic, and unattractive.
And once the shock effect has worn off
It is a mad repetition of silly sex.
Sexual freedom has at last been exposed
For the hoax it has always been.
The sexually free man can be seen
Drifting down Forty-second Street in New York,
Or the Tenderloin in San Francisco.
Viewing machines have now been installed
In his favorite dirty bookstore
Where for a quarter he can see
A five-minute parade of nudes,
Or he can step into the back room
And for one dollar see a continuous showing
Of frolicking nudes on wide screen.
And to satisfy his complete sexual freedom,
There is a supermarket-type display
Of pornographic books and magazines:
There is a handbook for every variety of obsession.
Why, then, is this sexually-liberated person
So bored with it all?

LOVING NEEDS CARE.
V.D. and Prenatal Health Care.
FREE! No questions asked.
Call County Hospital, Ext. 53.
Hurry.

—*Los Angeles Times*

His morality has been annihilated!
He has been smothered by flesh and anatomy;
        Anything goes.
Nothing is sinful,
        But look at him: sullen, limp-eyed, resigned.
He looks like he would trade it all for a good home-cooked
    meal
        And some bright conversation with a square.
If I were led by God to start an international war
        On pornography and sexual freedom,
I would enlist my army from the ranks
        Of those bored and lonely souls
        Who have already tired of it.
What zeal they would have, once they came to themselves.
        Their message is already coming through:

LIFE ON THE EDGE OF TIME

License does not insure liberty.

Nudity without purpose can become boring and even
ridiculous.

Pornography is an addiction of idiots.

Dirty movies are bad for the eyes as well as the soul.

Smut peddlers are giggling all the way to the bank.

Changing partners is neither fun nor free.

Unlimited sexual opportunity is nothing but vanity and
vexation.

It is a world of tragedy, grief, and guilt,

      Often ending in suicide.

God created sex, and only He can free it.

      It was declared once,

      For all generations to hear and heed.

      The marriage bed is undefiled:

      Sex outside marriage is doomed and damned.

Those whom God hath joined together

      In *holy* matrimony ARE FREE!

AESOP AND THE REVOLUTIONARY

Revolution is an overused word;
(No one today seems able to clarify it).
It was at one time the armed seizure of power.
But the revolutionary is now stereotyped:
He is young, bearded, and wears a fatigue jacket.
Sporting a beret, he clenches his fist like Fidel,
Carries a side arm,
And says dirty words on television.

 The smaller the mind, the greater the conceit.

He smokes pot,
And sleeps with rebel groupies.
They all promise peace, bread, and land.

 Beware the insincere friend.

The youngest of them are romantic Maoists and Fidelists.
Older ones are more historically minded,

Having read Marx, Lenin, and Trotsky.
The more sophisticated relate to
Rosa Luxemburg, Kuron, and Modzelewski—the Polish
    rebel.

    Beware the promises of a desperate man.

They talk about participatory democracy
And letting the people decide—
SDS and all New Left organizations cry:
"Give the power back to the people!"
So their organizers begin dragging people to meetings.
It creates a lot of excitement,
But when it wears off they run into
Michel's "iron law of obligatory"!

    The best liars often get caught in their own lies.

Power falls into the hands of a few rebel leaders.
Then, as the glamor fades away
A new generation of bureaucratic hack(s) is born.
People still have to be dragged to meetings,

Still refusing to participate:
Not wanting to get involved.
So the reform movement is crippled
By the same disease democracy suffers.

A level path is pleasing to the laden beast.

So groovy revolutionaries try to govern by decree,
All for the best interests of the masses.

Lean freedom is better than fat slavery.

By bullet or ballot,
They are determined to seize the power!
At times they succeed.
With boundless energy the New Left intellectuals move in
To end racism and exploitation,
To give all the land back to the people,
To control corporate structures.
But then comes the great reckoning: the moment of truth!
Modern technology has no mercy on revolutionaries.
Slogans and rhetoric can't run computers.

LIFE ON THE EDGE OF TIME

One good plan that works is better than a hundred
doubtful ones.

Steel mills and power plants demand
An elite corps of engineers and experts.
Behind a single yard of electric wiring
Lies a copper mine,

Stretch your arm no farther than your sleeve will reach.

The machinery needed to operate it,
Plants for producing insulating material,
Copper smelters,
Shaping complexes,
A transportation system to distribute it,
And behind these plants,
Other mines—complexes—machine shops,
And an army of workers
Who tire quickly of slogans.

Figures don't lie, but they won't make a hen lay.

They don't want cybernated industrial assembly lines
With baskets passed out at the end

To cart the goods home—free.
Men prefer the dignity of purchasing power.
Modern society is now so complex:

> The ignorant despise what is precious only because
> they cannot understand it.

Bogged down in mountains of paper work,
And all the revolutionaries
Have to bow in awe
To the bourgeois complexity—
Dossiers, filing systems, forms, punch cards.
The truth is:
Fidel Castro and other revolutionaries
All end up getting lost
In a maze of filing cabinets and typewriters.

> It is one thing to propose, another to execute.

Supersonic jets can't operate on people power.
Jolly, gaping tourists stay at home.
The sick and suffering turn to the skilled physicians.
Everyone wants at least two shoes!

LIFE ON THE EDGE OF TIME

Suddenly the rubbish of revolution is exposed.
The masses begin to notice:
They have been treated like a giant blob of dough,
Kneaded by one elite after another,
Thrown into the rebel's pan,
And carved and consumed
By the lust of men for power.

Treachery is the basest crime of all.

We can see the revolutionary for what he really is:
Just another demagogue,
Another money-mad capitalist,

A change of scene does not change one's character.

A new kind of self-styled dictator,
In different clothes,
Using different words,
To do the same old thing!

Magnificent promises often end in paltry performances.

So you can quit planting your bombs
And shaking your fist at me.
Quit putting me on about some dream

> Do not denounce the genuine, only to applaud an
> imitation.

Of a rural crash-pad without problems—
Where no one had to work.
Stop trying to free me from the system

> One man's meat is another man's poison.

So I can run off to some freak farm.
Revolution solves nothing:
It is just one bad man clubbing another.

> Liberty is too high a price to pay for revenge.

But there is an alternative.
It's called: the Kingdom of God.
It's a kind of heaven on earth
Based on love—one for another,

LIFE ON THE EDGE OF TIME

Being a channel of God's love,
Sharing and giving and trusting,
Because in God there is neither Jew nor Gentile,
Rich nor poor, black nor white.
We are all *one* in Christ,
Who believe and accept His claims.

> Throw no stones into the well that quenches your
> thirst.

The quotations in the above poem are from Aesop, a Greek
fabulist of the sixth century B.C.

WAR ON POLLUTION

There can be no high civility without a deep morality.

—Emerson

The Bible warns:
"For in much wisdom is much grief:
And he that increaseth knowledge increaseth sorrow."
Let me share knowledge that increases all our sorrow:

A population explosion endangers the earth.
To combat it, the pill is introduced.
Then we are warned it could clot the blood;
We are informed our drinking water is like refined
sewage;
Lake Erie is dead,
Streams everywhere are polluted,
The ocean is sick;
Air is loaded with deadly gases;
Noise pollution is affecting our hearing;

Automobiles are unsafe at any speed;
Certain animals are now extinct;
Nature is spinning out of balance.
Ralph Nader and the ecologists keep increasing my
knowledge
About every kind of pollution,
And my sorrow increases.
Not because I am afraid,
But because our values have become so perverted.
Millions will now be spent to fight physical pollution,
Nothing is spent to combat spiritual pollution.
Man has become alarmed about his environment
But refuses to admit his spirit is corrupted and abused.
Everything for ecology,
Nothing for theology.
Our pollution problem is the same as Sodom's:
Nakedness,
Adultery,
Homosexuality,
Permissiveness,
Lawlessness,
Materialism,
Love of pleasure.

Moral pollution is leading to spiritual cancer,
A conceived lust that brings forth death.
We suffer from the gain-is-godliness syndrome.
Everybody wants to make it big.
Success is determined by dollar bills,
       Swimming pools,
       Fancy cars.
We are breeding rich devils, but poor saints.
Playboy nudity is not our real enemy;
It is the lust of things creeping in and choking us.
Warned by God to flee these things,
Christians have instead become addicted to the good life.
       Corrupt conversation pollutes the soul.
       Evil communications spoil good manners.
       Four-letter words seem almost angelic
       Compared to the vitriolic gossip,
       The innuendoes,
       The character assassinations,
       And poisoned half-truths
       Spewing out of the mouths of brothers.
We need a Holy Ghost Mouthwash
Or at least a new kind of honesty
That would preface all gossip with an admission:

"This filth is brought to you
through the discourtesy of a
jealous, grudging, big mouth."
Yet the most fatal kind of pollution is the sin of unawareness.
Millions are snared and trapped by it.

They have put the coming of Christ out of mind,
Living in total disregard for His return.
This leads to loose living,
To divorce,
Boredom,
Too much leisure.
Life becomes a fun game,
A time to sleep,
While the world teeters on the brink of time.
The Bible warns,
"Watch ye therefore:
For ye know not when the master of the house
cometh . . .
Lest coming suddenly he find you sleeping,
And what I say unto you I say unto all,
Watch."
We can win this war on spiritual pollution,

For this is the victory that overcometh the world
    And its pollution—even our faith!

> Right and wrong aren't dropped from the sky. We
> make them. Against misery. Invariably misery follows
> their disobedience.

—John Updike, Rabbit, Run

THE SOUND IS ROCK

The sound is rock,
  But it all means *money*!
Album jackets call artists revolutionaries.
  Rock stars wail in anger,
  Screaming revolt and subversion—
  Then leave concerts in Cadillacs.
Rock music has become a financial staple
  Of U.S. Wall Street imperialism.
The money octopus has a strangle-hold
  On the singing rebel.
This society has already absorbed
  All the rebellion and sexuality it can stand.
Reconversion is essential
  But probably impossible.
Even though there is no rock in Congress,
  It is very economically important.
Rock music has been subversive:
  A component of cross-class rebel youth culture.

Yet Madison Avenue keeps trying to capture it
    And package it,
    And sell it.

    In a capitalist society everything is for sale—not only
    food, clothing, and shelter, but even songs.

                                        —A student

Rock is raw sex.
    It is a plea about loneliness.
It is young people trying to reach out
    Over barriers of personal isolation.
Rock is the energy of destruction
    Turning concerts into riot zones.
It may never be suppressed,
    "For it is exclusively ours," say the young.
The frenzy of rock
    Bulges the capitalistic pockets of record companies.
And I suspect that its purveyors
    Are not rebels or anti-Establishment people,
    But hip imperialists making a buck:
Ripping off kids with gut music
    Not to get a message across,

But to generate sales.

It is a phony extortion trip.

Pretending to generate radicalism,

They promote the rock star's image

As tough, unkempt, drugged, pig-hating!

And it's all just a money machine.

> Rock may have come from the streets, but in between
> you and the performer is billions of dollars. . . .
> Record companies make their money on antiwar youth
> culture.
>
> —Mark Kramer

Woodstock was not a festival:

It was a movie.

It was three million record albums.

It was television rights.

It was radical fall-out rhythm.

For sale!

The hucksters were all there.

So look here, all you rock lovers,

Don't knock my hymns—

They're still free!

I HAVE NOTHING, MA,
TO LIVE UP TO

"Blow your mind" is the rallying cry
        Of the new rebels and freedom fighters.
It is roughly equivalent to the cry
        Of an older historical period:
        "Break your chains, man."
This was Bob Dylan's message to the young,
        "You have nothing to lose but your mind."
They were invited to escape with him
        Into a world of dangerous fantasies,
        With no limitations on consciousness.
To achieve this freedom,
        They had to escape from historical values:
        And to transcend them, drugs were used.
In "Tambourine Man," Dylan wrote an ode
To drugs and the process of mind blowing:

And take me disappearing
Through the smoke rings of my mind,
Down the foggy ruins of time. . . .
Let me forget about today
Until tomorrow.

But on this road to freedom
        Many got lost along the way.
With the destruction of old values
        No new ones were created.
Because creation of new values
        Is hardly a sufficient goal for the political activists,
        No direct answers are attempted.
The mission of the radical is to escape:

                How does it feel?
                How does it feel
                To be on your own,
                With no direction home,
                Like a complete unknown,
                Like a rolling stone?

                                —Dylan

A new society is not almost here;
    But the old one seems to be breaking up.
Perhaps the kids who buy all those records
    Featuring vicious antinationalism
Really don't care about the content of the songs.
    (You can hardly understand the words anyhow.)
They hear only the sound of the beat.
    It pounds out but a single message:
    Blow your mind!
Walk over to your local high school.
    Watch them walk out,
    So many look like exiles,
    Baptized in private fantasies.
    What a tragedy,
Because Bob Dylan spun clear out
    Into a big pink mansion
    Celebrating the diseased life he once condemned.
A real down home commuter,
    Playing all the games he once put down.
My silly question is this:
    Why did he call me a work freak?
Hitching a ride on life's hang-ups,
    He sang himself into a legend,

LIFE ON THE EDGE OF TIME

Begging for mind blowups
      Only to cleverly cop out.
Wriggling free of past poems and songs
      To get hung-up in a silence conspiracy.
It leads to only one comment:
      Make no mystical pilgrimages into the mind
      To find the root-source of life.
Awareness and enjoyment spring from elsewhere—
      From Christ,
      The wellspring of life.

        Though the masters make the rules
        For the wise men and fools,
        I have nothing, Ma,
        To live up to.

                —Dylan

BLACK RAGE

~~~~~~

The once servile black masses are standing up,
And I am told:
     "We'd all better duck."
A conflagration is coming,
So state the writers,
     Unless whites get off the backs of blacks.
Rage is rising!

    Blacks bent double by oppression have stored up
    energy which will be released in the form of rage—
    Black Rage, apocalyptic and final.

Since one does not negotiate with servants,
Black men knew there had to be a transfer of power.
     The postal-worker syndrome had to be broken.
Blacks contaminated by fear
Had to be decontaminated
     And educated to the value of honest rebellion.

The young blacks fought back first.
(Their elders gave approval, but have not yet joined in.)

> Something just happened to the black people of the
> United States. We are no longer what we were a few
> years ago. Something has happened to us—to us, not
> America—something which is affecting our way of
> thinking. It is that fear has disappeared. We are no
> longer afraid to die. Now the white man is afraid.
> Now he is obliged to redefine his relationship with us.

> —The Reverend Cleage, Linwood Avenue Church

Small black drops of Negro freedom are not enough!
And all the sullen Afro-American youths
Who raise the black-power fist
        Remind us of the scars of prejudice.
The cancer of slavery
        Now takes its toll!
Black men will never again be satisfied
To do white man's dirty work:
        They have earned the right to self-development.
Better still, it is their birthright.

> The hippies, the yippies—we're niggers all, man. The
> hippies and yippies are trying to break out of the
> system and work their way down, and we're trying to
> break in and work up. And when we meet . . .
> America will die. It will die in 18 months. . . .
>
> —Dick Gregory

There is a current breaking of America into two parts.
It is a black-white encounter.
Rap Brown and Stokely Carmichael were products
      Made in America.
Their angry young lives demonstrate the fact
Our nation has not comprehended their message.
      White rhetoric and black ragings only fan the fire.
No honest Christian white man can deny
The oppression and condescension heaped on the black man.
As God's child he cannot indulge in prejudice—
      Even though some so-called saints despise blacks.
But black rage is out of control.
It now even consumes black ministers,
Turning men of God into demagogues
      Who threaten—and accuse—and terrorize,

And nothing can make it right.
Centuries of abuse cannot justify revenge:
>"Vengeance is mine . . . saith the Lord."

Men who walk with God will never be cowered
By threats or by warnings
From black men or white men
>Who practice prejudice in reverse.

I am not at all alarmed by the rhetoric
Of young black militants and Black Panthers.
>I will not be ducking for any of them.

But I am concerned
With black rage in the pulpit,
>By ministers of the Almighty,

Who speak words of violence,
Who turn brother against brother
>And use their black skin as a weapon.

I challenge all black rage in the house of God:
>It is not rooted in God's Word.

>It is not born out of love.

>It is not edifying and unifying!

Let every black brother remember his weapons are not
carnal:

The battle belongs to God.
We are all members of one body—
Not black or white,
But washed in Christ's blood.
We are commanded to love one another:
Black rage—white rage—is forbidden.

CHILDREN OF THE BOMB!

We are in the first phase of what is perhaps the pen-ultimate revolution. Its next phase may be atomic warfare.

—Aldous Huxley

There is no predictable future for them
    Living under the burden of change.
Confusion everywhere, verging on total chaos,
    No center to things—no shared belief.
To call it a revolution is too simple:
    Something is happening deeper than that.
It touches every aspect of life:
    Sex, religion, politics, and all the senses.
It is multidimensional and mysterious.
        In some way it has to do with rediscovering
        ONESELF,

Along with a foyer
    Into the mystery of the cosmos.
These youth are a class—a tribal class:
    Thinking of themselves as exploited, abused,
      processed.

    Things are in the saddle and they ride mankind.

                    —Emerson

Believing elders have failed them,
    They learn from one another.
They despise the old traditional ways of life
    Claiming they led to cesspools in Vietnam and
      Chicago.
Stubbornly determined not to be ruled by anyone,
    They repudiate most of the basic assumptions of
      society.
Down on all systems that stimulate greed,
    Sex desires that cannot be satisfied,
Hatred with no outlet but in violence,
    They feel like prisoners on this earth:
Worrying about their impotence to change things
    With no one to comfort them about tomorrow.

LIFE ON THE EDGE OF TIME

We see all around us a terrible alienation of the best
and bravest of our young; the very shape of a genera-
tion seems turned on its head overnight.

—The late Robert Kennedy

Phony religion only intensifies their confusion;
      Easy and early sexuality swallowed them up;
They were trapped in a web of new ideas;
      Drugs became a way out of the jungle—
      An escape from institutions geared to another
      generation.
They were unable to change the Establishment through rage,
      So they tried to melt into a landscape of fantasy;
      Through psychedelic adventures find a new
      revelation.
Hoping to discard their old identity and take on another,
      A strange kind of brotherhood developed
      With promise of dramatic and enchanting forms of
      reality.
Drug abuse became a shared experience—
      A group ride into risky currents.

PRESIDENT SAYS DRUGS NO. 1 PROBLEM

LIFE ON THE EDGE OF TIME

But the feeling of freedom was empty
>When all believable authority dissolved
And everything was replaced by experimental experience
>This false freedom was unmasked and exposed.
They had become gods to themselves
>Free souls took to the mountains and deserts.
They ran from God, from homes and parents,
>Simply hitchhiking or riding freight trains . . . away
>Just to see what lies beyond the next hill.
All the guides to life were lost or abandoned.
>That is how it happened.
Beginning in the early sixties
>We began to reap the failure of the fifties.
The children of the bomb suddenly split—
>Acidheads and potheads replaced eggheads.
Junkies and rebels became heroes.
>It became a "high" society
>Whose members turned from Billy Graham to Timothy Leary.
Dropping out became a religious experience—
>Hard kicks replaced soft kicks:
>Young people flirted with the outer perimeter of existence.

LIFE ON THE EDGE OF TIME

Flights from reality chipped away at their hearts
           Emptying them of hope and belief;
Life became nothing but an empty outline.
Eaten with an inner intensity they could not name,
           Children of the bomb lived with absolute
              annihilation
Spreading that indelible stain on everything they touched.
           World crises and assassinations and civil wars
All brought new feelings of alienation and hopelessness.

> Are we witnessing the final act of a Greek tragedy,
> with the chorus warning of the impending disaster, but
> helpless to act? Maybe we are.
>
>   —Erich Fromm

The hypocrisy of high dignitaries
           And the immorality of the new world church
Cut them off from the root-source of life.
The children of the bomb have been radicalized
           Introduced by the underground to one view of issues.
Tossing insults at nonliberated people,
           They have become polarized and crystalized;

A nation within a nation,
>Clustered in big city Bohemias,
>"Love is alive and hiding in San Francisco"

Fighting off malnutrition and VD
>Migrating across continents,

Fleeing from an unnamed enemy,
>Seeking an undefined haven,

Running from the bosom of middle-class obesity,
>Tired of superficial fashion hang-ups
>Promoted by dollar-mad manufacturers,

They parade in curious costumes and wild dress,
>Blasting intellectuals, liberals, and the Establishment alike.

Unwilling to punch a clock for industry
>(While their fathers sever the tie between work and wages)

Their nervous systems have been shattered
>By news media panic and rumors of war.

So they have turned to a romantic infatuation with guerrilla warfare:
>A misty-eyed involvement in power struggles,
>Enchantment with the teaching of Mao and Che Guevara.

CRIES OF 'CHE' TAUNT VICE-PRESIDENT AGNEW

They feel the empire is crumbling
     As did all others in history.
So the continents are up for grabs.
     They believe the country is coming down
     And will die off like an insect.
So they want to go down making love,
     And singing in the face of the apocalypse.
You see this new breed sitting in hordes all over the world
     Waiting for a suicidal, killer world to end.

       ". . . blood, and fire, and pillars of smoke."

                 —Joel, the prophet

Not a word has to be spoken between them.
     It is an inner message they have all received:
     THE END IS NEAR,
And organized religion doesn't have a ghost of a chance
     To reach them in their bankruptcy.
     All hope is gone—every door shut.
Except One!
     JESUS CHRIST—THE SOLID ROCK

He is now restoring—uniting—healing.
    His presence is now an international issue.
Thousands of revolutionaries have been captured by Him!
    Christ is whacking the powers that be!
    Change is in the air!
False clergymen are sweating in their starchy collars,
    While a Jesus phenomenon punctures their dogma.
Mao's Red bible is being exchanged for God's Holy Bible.
    There is even a stirring in the dirt:
Junkies, harlots, hippies, and freaks
    Now preach, praise, and pray.
JESUS CHRIST, SUPERFRIEND
    Has replaced Jesus Christ Superstar.
Heaven's Western Union has telegraphed a message,
    And the children of the bomb are receiving it
    Loud and clear:
Jesus Christ will soon return
    To enlist an army of believers,
Raptured in the twinkling of an eye
    To meet Him midair in the cosmos.
And it shall be even as the Scriptures promise:
    Whosoever will call upon the name of the Lord
    Shall be saved.

LIFE ON THE EDGE OF TIME

This really revolutionary revolution is to be achieved, not in the external world, but in the souls and flesh of human beings.

—Aldous Huxley

A LETTER FROM THE APOSTLE PAUL

For the Lord himself will come down from heaven
with a mighty shout and with the soul-stirring
    cry . . .
and the great trumpet-call of God.
. . . the believers who are dead will be the first
    to rise. . . .
Then we who are alive and remain . . .
will be caught up with them in the clouds
to meet the Lord in the air. . . .
When is all this going to happen?
. . . you know perfectly well that no one knows.
That day of the Lord will come unexpectedly
like a thief in the night.
When people are saying, "All is well,
everything is quiet and peaceful"—
then, all of a sudden, disaster will fall . . .
as suddenly as a woman's birth pains begin
when her child is born.

. . . people will not be able to get away any-
   where—
there will be no place to hide.
But, dear brothers, you are not in the dark
about these things. . . .
So be on your guard,
not asleep like the others.
Watch for his return
and stay sober.
For God has not chosen to pour out his anger
   upon us,
but to save us through our Lord Jesus Christ;
he died for us so we can live with him . . .
whether we are dead or alive at the time of his
   return.
Do not scoff at those who prophesy. . . .
Keep away from every kind of evil.
. . . may your spirit and soul and body be kept
   blameless
until that day when our Lord Jesus Christ comes
   back. . . .

Sincerely,

Paul

I Thessalonians, Chapters 4, 5 (TLB)

ALPHABET SOUP

~~~~~~

The revolution is drowning in alphabet soup.
You just can't project yourself today—
      Or your message—
Without the alphabet!
Raise a single issue today—and a dozen more groups get
   in the soup.
Stop me when you've had enough.

SDS	(Students for Democratic Society)
ADA	(Americans for Democratic Action)
NOW	(National Organization for Women)
WITCH	(Woman's International Terrorists Conspiracy From Hell)
WRL	(War Resisters League)
LNS	(Liberation News Service)
UPS	(Underground Press Syndicate)
MCHR	(Medical Committee for Human Rights)

PRAC   (Poverty Rights Action Group)

PAR   (People Against Racism)

CLU   (Civil Liberties Union)

DRV   (Democratic-Republic Revolution in
                Vermont)

BTU   (Berkely Tenants Union)

SA   (Schizophrenics Anonymous)

SFL   (Sexual Freedom League)

GLL   (Gay Liberation League)

CIPA   (Committee for Independent Political
                Action)

SAMDS   (Springfield Area Movement for a Demo-
                cratic Society)

SNCC   (Student Nonviolent Coordinating Com-
                mittee)

SSOC   (Southern Student Organizing Committee)

NUC   (New University Conference)

PIG   (Politics in General)

YES   (Youth Equality Services)

NO	(No [we won't go] Organization)
CCC	(Communist Coordinating Committee)
SSS	(Social Students Society)
RRR	(Radicals-Revolutionaries-in Rebellion)
CAROTC	(Committee Against Reserve Officers Training Corps)
HSSRC	(High School Student Right Coalition)
SMC	(Student Movement Coordinator)
TWM	(Third World Movement)
CFHN	(Committee to Free Huey Newton)
UMAS	(United Mexican American Students)
RP	(Radicals in the Professions)
YLO	(Young Lords Organization)
RUA	(Rising Up Angry)
SCAR	(Southern Committee Against Repression)
LRBW	(League of Revolutionary Black Workers)

The revolution may never die from lack of issues
It will simply run out of alphabet.

FROM ADAM'S RIB TO WOMAN'S LIB

What in the world is woman's lib?
I am told it is simply organized rage
Against the oppression of females:

> The woman's movement must define itself in terms of
> itself. We must find our history and create it. Fifty-
> three percent of the population is women, and the key
> to everyone else's liberation.

> —Rosaglem Baxandall, New York Radical Women

The family system is now considered by them
To be a capitalistic tool to suppress females.
The women are being organized
So they will no longer be the slaves of men.
Hear the "Redstocking Manifesto" of July 7, 1969:

> Women are an oppressed class. Our oppression is
> total, affecting every facet of our life. We are ex-

ploited as sex objects, breeders, domestic servants and cheap labor. We are considered inferior beings whose only purpose is to enhance men's lives. Our humanity is denied. Our prescribed behavior is enforced by the threat of physical violence.

So—they have identified the agents of their oppression:
The dominant, racist, sexist, egoist male.
They say all men have oppressed all women.
Lib groups reject the idea
That women consent to or are to blame for
Their own oppression.
They are not out to change women—but men.
Their chief task is to publicly expose
The sexist foundation of all our institutions.

> We call on all our sisters to unite
> with us in this struggle. We call on
> all men to give up their male privileges
> and support woman's lib in the interest
> of our humanity and their own. The time
> for individual skirmishes is over: This
> time we are going all the way.
> —Redstocking Manifesto

Woman's lib pictures women lying on society's shelf
As damaged goods,
Dehumanized, dependent, deprived, and discouraged
By having to bear the image of being stupid.
Go into the mind of lib-leaning women
And here is what you find:

> I am confined to my house, a chauffeur to my kids, a maid to my man. My husband goes out into the real world. Other people recognize him as real. They take him into account. He does things and changes things. I stay in my imaginary world. In this house, doing jobs I invent. No one cares about them but myself. I do not change things. The work I do changes nothing. The food I cook disappears. What I clean one day must be cleaned again the next. If my husband stops loving me, I'm sunk. I would have no purpose in life. I have to depend on him. I would be nothing by myself.
>
> —From "The Divided Self" by Laing

I am a man.
I want to confess

LIFE ON THE EDGE OF TIME

To woman's lib, to my wife, and to all women:
You have been taken for granted.
Men often do act like warlords.
We have not had confidence
You could do important things.
You have served men more than God demands.
Our male egos have been built by dwarfing yours.
We have not understood your trapped feeling.
Your rights have been impinged on,
And you should be free of all this oppression.
But God has something to say about woman's lib:
Don't use sex as a weapon or an excuse.
The man has been set by God
As head of the house with a command to love his wife
As Christ loved His church.
And to His church, God said,
       You are no longer servants,
       But heirs and joint-heirs.
       You are one—in spirit and flesh.

THE HOUR HAS COME

Let this generation hear what Christ said:
The hour has come . . . and now is. . . .
That I must fall to the ground and die
Like a kernel of wheat.
This He said to barbarian Greeks who informed the disciples,
"We would see Jesus."
The hour had come,
All seekers were told to meet Him at the cross.

> Cheap grace is the deadly enemy of our Church. We
> are fighting today for costly grace.

No more loaves and fishes.
No more "prove me" miracles to induce faith.
No more curiosity seeking.
No more answers to Pharisaical questions or science riddles.
Jesus told His disciples to tell the Greeks:

The Master is headed for Calvary—to die.
You must fall on the ground and die also.

> Cheap grace means grace as a doctrine, a principle,
> a system. Cheap grace is the preaching of forgiveness
> without requiring repentance.

Our message today is still one of dying:
No cheap revelations of Christ through drugs,
No promises to fulfill visions of a better world,
For God is not fooled by seekers who do nothing but seek.
The crowd once sought Him for the loaves and fishes;
Others followed to consume Him upon themselves,
Unwilling to share Him with a dying world.

> Cheap grace is grace without discipleship, grace with-
> out the cross, grace without Jesus Christ, living and
> incarnate.

Now there is only one way to see Jesus;
Every barbarian, every intellectual, every harlot,
All must come the same way,
Meeting Him at the same place.

He can be found only at Calvary—through dying.
The Bible says,
This is the generation that seeketh after Him.

> Costly grace is the gospel which must be *sought* again
> and again, the gift which must be *asked* for, the door
> at which a man must *knock*.

Phillip, the evangelist who won an entire city for Christ
Could not handle the problem of the barbarian Greeks
Who came seeking Christ.
Phillip told Andrew about it.
The two of them told Jesus about it.
How do you minister to seeking barbarians?
Even Andrew, the personal worker, seemed baffled
By these polluters of the temple
Who insisted on seeing only Jesus.

> Such grace is *costly* because it calls us to follow, and
> it is *grace* because it calls us to follow *Jesus Christ*. It
> is costly because it costs a man his life, and it is grace
> because it gives a man the only true life.

LIFE ON THE EDGE OF TIME

But the hour had come.
No one could see Him now,
Unless they too were ready to die;
To crucify the old man by faith;
To take up a cross and follow Him;
Despising the life of selfishness and pride;
Exchanging it for eternal life.
He must become a way of dying
Before He can become a way of living.

> The above quotations are from the young German Christian, Dietrich Bonhoeffer in *The Cost of Discipleship*. These words fell on deaf ears, for the German church chose rather to comply with Adolf Hitler's Nazis. Bonhoeffer was abandoned by church friends, and was shortly thereafter imprisoned by the Gestapo. He was executed by special order of Himmler on April 9, 1945. No costlier grace could be found. Bonhoeffer was first and last a man for Jesus.

BRICK BOXES

It is an illusion
>That the most important learning happens in school

School has become a ritual of certification

A kind of badge for success
>Almost a strange kind of religion

With worshipers bowing to a diploma
>We invest twelve years of schooling in each student

At a cost of between ten and eighteen thousand dollars
>Thirteen thousand hours behind a desk

>At more than one dollar per hour

It has become a mad cult
>With a ritual all its own

Children are forced to sit five hours a day
>Five days a week

>Ten months a year

For a minimum of twelve years

People have failed to justify why we are going to
school. They have never satisfactorily answered the
question: Why are we sending students to school?
They don't know why! This is why kids are destroyed
in school, because no one really knows why you are
going. Why are you taking math? Why algebra two?
Why are you taking calculus? You do it so you can get
a better job. You go to college, get that better job,
make more money, buy a car, be a consumer. The
horrible thought is that maybe there is no justifica-
tion for our doing all this. Maybe we're going up a
wrong alley.

—Steve

The student is graded, upgraded and downgraded
He is taught to believe dropouts are doomed to failure
        Graduates guaranteed success
Even garbage collectors have to have their diploma now
        We spread this same educational gospel around the
            world
        And unable to afford it
        We make them feel they are inferior—uneducated

Yet in America our schools are stultifying many students
    Who just manage to pass through.

    All you need to get through school nowadays is a good
    memory.

                                              —Judy

    When the bell rings—everybody runs for that door.
                                              —Fred

    School is a long lesson on how to turn yourself off.
                                              —John Holt

Our most educated students now turn to drugs
They leave home and curse society
        Brilliantly educated kids become agnostics and
            unpatriotic

    The high school is a reflection of the society which
    created high schools. If you think schools are sick—

LIFE ON THE EDGE OF TIME

look at society. High schools have lost their meaning.
They've become a sort of halfway house for wayward
boys and girls on their way to college or the draft . . .

—Steve

Education has become a tonic of madness
       For students crammed with unprocessed knowledge

Here is this nice little sterile cubicle, and you turn your
mind off when you get inside. What goes on in class
has nothing to do with the world, and they call this
learning. . . .

—Jim Boulet

We need to get kids out of the school buildings, give
them a chance to learn about the world at first hand.
It is a very recent idea, and a crazy one, that the way
to teach our young people about the world they live in
is to take them out of it and shut them up in brick
boxes.

—John Holt

LIFE ON THE EDGE OF TIME

So now the entire education system
    Is chewing itself with revolt
Kids are getting wise
        They don't want to be pumped through a system
           like a product
        Being jammed with dull facts
        While being pitted against each other for grades
           and rank
Right answers are all the school wants
And a student learns countless strategies
To con teachers into thinking he knows what he doesn't
   know
        A student spends most of his time outguessing and
           pleasing teachers
Rather than expanding his mind
        He learns to dodge, to bluff, fake and cheat
He learns to be lazy—to goldbrick
        He learns how to be bored—to daydream
Back in kindergarten he learned
        Teachers only love children who stand in nice
           straight lines
And that's where it's been ever since
        Fear of bad grades leads to blind obedience

LIFE ON THE EDGE OF TIME

Every low grade is torture
Students break out in pimples—
      Their bowels boil
It is like the last judgment
And students learn to hate all it stands for.

> I had a dream last night, that my math teacher failed
> me. I went up to him and punched him in the nose.
> Then I just kept on beating him until he was out cold.
> Then I stuck a great big pin in him and let all the air
> out of him. . . .
>
> —From "The Real World"

> The thing I object to so much in schools is that all
> they do is prepare you for tests and the tests are testing
> you on what you don't know. They're not testing you
> on what you do know. . . .
>
> —Kathryn

There has to be an alternative
But free street universities are not the answer

> Write today for your free catalogue:
> Midpenninsula Free University

Menlo Park, California
Our intriguing courses include:
Zombie Drawing
Pool Playing
Swedish Massage
Hitchhiking
Birdwatching
Breast Feeding
Magic Mushrooms
Insanity and Genius
Pig Law

Young people no longer want to learn answers
Because the answers keep changing so fast now
They are more interested in how to cope with life
      And they are tired of being graded like eggs
Education needs to be rescued
      From the death grip of bureaucratics
It is time to stop engineering our kids into social molds
      Perpetuated by the PTA
God help our kids
      If we keep on experimenting with them
While at the same time making God out as a villain

LIFE ON THE EDGE OF TIME

God help our kids.
      If teachers lose their dedication
While grabbing for dollars
The least we can do is welcome God back into the system
He knows when He is wanted or needed
      And we sure do need Him now

GOD WELCOME HERE

      (Third grade sign, Dallas)

The system would have its heart back
      And even if there were no miracles involved
      Love would return
For God is love
And love covers a multitude of sins
Kids respond to it
      And learn by it
      And grow by it
And the Brick Box would at least have a new window
      So the light could shine in.
        "I am the Light of the world."

BEWARE OF PHONY JESUS PEOPLE

The Bible predicts:
>Satan will attempt to infiltrate
>The Jesus restoration movement
>>With PHONIES.

NOW HEAR THIS:

Not everyone who uses My name
>Will enter the kingdom of heaven—
>But he that doeth the will of my Father.

Yet many will come on that final day saying,
>"Lord, we preached in your name!"
>"We did miracles in Jesus' name!"
>"We cast out devils!"
>"We did many wonderful works!"

But the Lord will say to them,
>"Depart from me, you indulgers in sin.
>I never ever knew you."

Woe unto you, hypocrites and Pharisees!

You pretend to be holy
    With your long public demonstrations and prayers.
You try to look saintly and pious,
    But under your robes you are besmirched
    With every sort of hypocrisy and sin.
You go to all lengths
    To make one convert,
    Then turn him into twice the son of hell you are.
You tithe and keep the law to the last letter,
    But you forget the more important things:
    Justice, Mercy, and Faith.
You strain at gnats and swallow camels.
    You polish the outside,
    But the inside is foul and corrupt.
False prophets shall arise and lead many astray,
    Doing wonderful miracles—
    Attempting to deceive even God's elect.
I have warned you:
    By their fruits you shall know them—
    Where there is confusion and division
    There is evil work.
You would think these phonies were Moses

The way they keep making up so many laws
And making people obey their every whim.
DON'T follow their example!
They load you with impossible demands,
And don't try to keep them themselves.
All they do is for show
The true test is LOVE.
For if any man love not his brother,
The love of God is not in him.
He is a phony!

THE JESUS RESTORATION MOVEMENT

The prophet Joel predicted
     Immediately prior to the coming of Christ
An army of Jesus people would be raised up
     To prepare the way
Commissioned to make a midnight cry
     "Go out and meet Him"

He described this army (Joel 2):

     They will sound an alarm that judgment is near
     A great and powerful army
     The likes of them have not been seen before
     And never will again
     Upsetting the calm and peace of the land
     Marching, like mounted warriors
     A fire raging across the fields
     The world will not understand them
     Charging like infantry men

Climbing over obstacles like commandoes
Refusing to break rank, never crowding one another
Each person right in his place
One chief commander, God
They swarm over cities, mountains, walls
Shaking things up
Shining so brightly they obscure the sun and stars
The Lord leads them with a shout
They obey His orders
Knowing the day of the Lord has come
And no one can endure that awesome day

They all preach one message:

Turn to the Lord Christ
While there is time
Give Him all your heart
Come and surrender to Him
Repent and change your life
He is merciful and kind
Full of forgiveness and love
He does not want to punish or hurt you
So He calls you in love

LIFE ON THE EDGE OF TIME

Whosoever shall call upon His name
Shall be saved.

Now drug abusers quit using narcotics
       Potheads and acid-freaks study their Bibles
       Runaways and hippies turn to the Lord
Student agnostics and atheists open their minds
       Inviting Jesus Christ in
            Why did it happen so suddenly?
            Why is it spreading to every nation?
            What does it all mean?
            What miracle has happened?
       Former junkies and prostitutes stand on street
          corners
       Warning men to repent and prepare
       Converted hippies and freaks invade every sector
          of society
       Warning of coming judgment
Our forefathers would never have believed
       Such a thing could happen—
It is a deluge of the Holy Spirit
       On the face of this earth
The return of Jesus Christ is right at the door

When the Holy Spirit is poured out
> Three things happen
>> He convinces every human being of his sin
>> He reveals the availability of God's grace
>> He convinces men of certain coming
>>> judgment
>> "And when he has come [the Holy Spirit]
>> he will
>> Convince the world of its sin,
>> and of the availability
>> of God's goodness,
>> and of deliverance from judgment. . . ."
>>> (TLB)

The Holy Spirit is overwhelming nations
> Moslems and Jews experience it
> Politicians, world leaders and dictators
> Rich and poor—black, white, red and yellow
> Criminals
> Prostitutes
> Students, professors, ministers, labor leaders
> The old and feeble—the young and strong
> Russians, Chinese, Africans, Indians and Europeans

Every person must either respond or reject

LIFE ON THE EDGE OF TIME

The rejectors will say:
"But where is the sign of His coming
For things continue as they were
From the beginning of time."
They will become pleasure-mad and sensuous
Laughing at the thought of judgment and death
They will turn to an Antichrist
Filling the earth with sex, perversion, crime and
violence.
Those who respond become new people
It will all end in the twinkling of an eye
The trumpet of God will sound
Christ will appear in the heavens
To evacuate His children from the earth
The Holy Spirit will end His work
We who trust and believe will vanish
Our vile bodies will be exchanged
For glorious new ones
God gave us certain clues
Pinpointing the general time of Christ's return
He gave us the Noah sign
Drunkards and gluttons
Playing games of marriage and divorce

Great prosperity—a construction boom
Absorbed in trade, merchandise
And fashion
The Peace sign
Men shall cry peace—peace and safety
Then shall the end come
Men will cry and sigh to live in safety
From bombs, threats, wars and rumors of wars
Thousands have joined the peace movements
The Violence sign
Men will
Despise government
Riot in the daytime and speak evil of those in
authority
Speak swelling words of vanity
Seduce the innocent and mock righteousness
Flirt with evil powers and demons
Live in sin while sitting in on the Jesus feasts
Proudly boast of their perversion and sin
These things are all reflected in today's newspaper
The clues are all in
The last call has gone out
Will you be ready to go when He comes?

The Bible warns:

> "I tell you, in that night
> there shall be two men in one bed;
> the one shall be taken, and the other shall be left.
> Two women shall be grinding together;
> the one shall be taken, and the other left.
> Two men shall be in the field;
> the one shall be taken, and the other left.
>
> Be ye therefore ready also for the Son of
> man cometh at an hour when ye
> think not.